# ROBERT SMALLS
# AMERICAN HERO

# ROBERT F. KENNEDY, JR.

### Illustrations by Patrick Faricy

Sky Pony Press
New York

## ACKNOWLEDGMENTS

My gratitude to my extraordinarily talented researcher Brendan DeMelle, and to Mary Beth Postman, who organizes my life so that I have time to read history and write books for children, and to my assistant Lori Morash, who can somehow read my chicken scratch, and to Donna Bray at Hyperion, who helps to make this endeavor so fun.

Text copyright ©2008, 2023 by Robert F. Kennedy, Jr.

Illustrations and map copyright ©2008, 2023 by Patrick Faricy

First Sky Pony Press Edition 2023

Sky Pony Press books may be purchased in bulk at special discounts for sales promotion, corporate gifts, fund-raising, or educational purposes. Special editions can also be created to specifications. For details, contact the Special Sales Department, Sky Pony Press, 307 West 36th Street, 11th Floor, New York, NY 10018 or info@skyhorsepublishing.com.

Sky Pony® is a registered trademark of Skyhorse Publishing, Inc.®, a Delaware corporation.

Visit our website at www.skyponypress.com.

10 9 8 7 6 5 4 3 2

Library of Congress Cataloging-in-Publication Data is available on file.

Cover design by Kai Texel
Cover illustration by Dennis Nolan

Print ISBN: 978-1-5107-7834-4
Ebook ISBN: 978-1-5107-7909-9

Printed in China

To my friend John Lewis and the other
old warhorses who never stop fighting for the
noble ideal of Robert Smalls' America.
— *Robert F. Kennedy, Jr.*

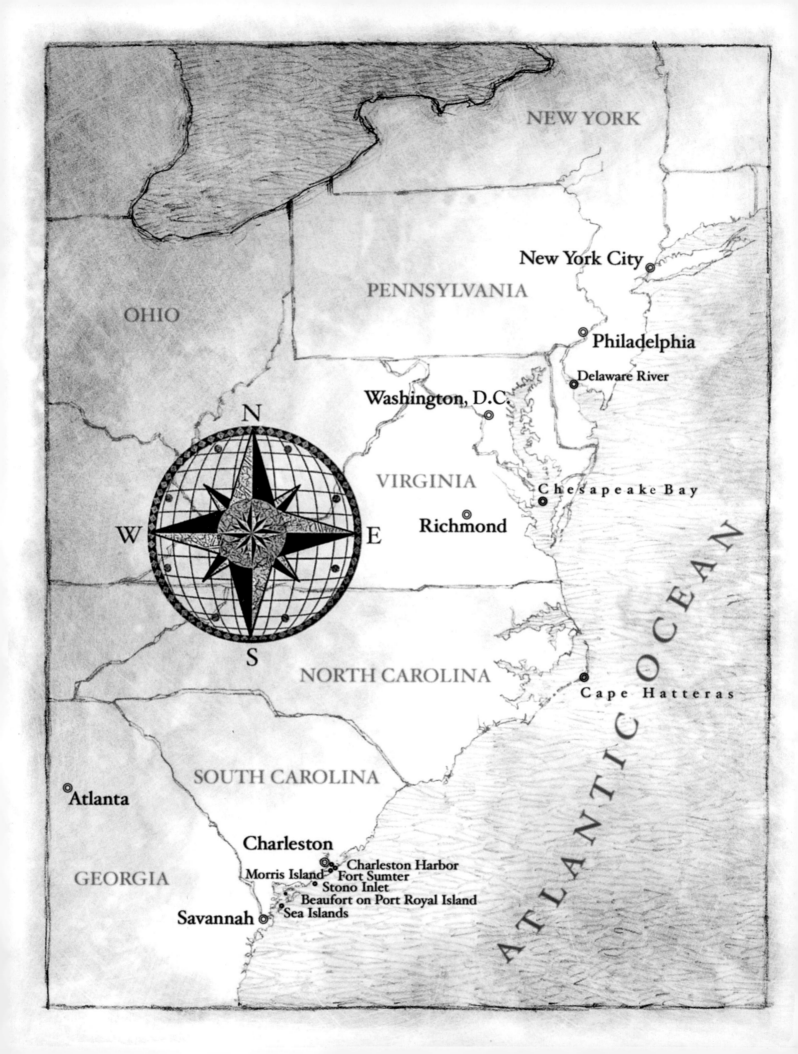

# CONTENTS

Introduction / vii

1   House Slave and Sailor / 1

2   The *Planter* / 5

3   Sailing to Freedom / 9

4   Back on Shore / 15

5   The Battle for Stono Inlet / 17

6   Captain Robert Smalls / 20

7   Abe Lincoln / 25

8   Philadelphia / 28

9   Home to Beaufort / 30

10   The Confederacy Rises Again / 34

Afterword / 39

Bibliography / 40

# INTRODUCTION

In the spring of 1862, the world was watching the South Carolina port of Charleston. One year earlier, the Confederate bombardment of Fort Sumter had launched the American Civil War. Confederate forces now occupied Fort Sumter and the many fortified islands guarding the Rebel harbor. The Union had enjoyed very little good news since the Confederate seizure of Charleston.

Then, on a moonlit May night, nine Black slaves, in a daring gambit, stole the Confederate's prize gunship as it lay tied to the wharf in front of Confederate headquarters in Charleston Harbor and ran the port's heavily armed gauntlet of outer fortifications and battlements, delivering the vessel to the American navy. The warship, a giant side-wheel steamer called the *Planter*, was the fastest ship in the harbor. She was the pride of Charleston and the most important ship in the local Rebel fleet. The daring slaves had commandeered her from under the noses of twenty-one Confederate troops guarding her from just a few feet away.

The brassy getaway riveted the globe and enraged the Confederate government. The loss of their finest ship, with its irreplaceable cannons and ordnance, was both a military disaster and a humiliating blow to Rebel morale. Even worse, the audacious and intricately coordinated escape exploded the Confederate claim that Southern slaves did not crave freedom and were incapable of decisive and deliberate action.

The bold feat of intricate planning and courageous execution at the birthplace of the Civil War electrified Northern states weary from the parade of grim battlefield dispatches. Northern papers praised "the audacious Africans" for their gallantry. The *New York Times* proclaimed the deed "one of the most heroic acts of the war." The plot's ringleader—an illiterate slave sailor named Robert Smalls—became a national hero. Editorial pages argued that Smalls had proven that Black slaves were ready for full freedom and citizenship. The *New York Daily Tribune* asked, "What White man has made a bolder dash or won a richer prize in the teeth of such perils during the war?" The paper added that Smalls' actions had demonstrated that "Negro slaves have skill and courage. They will risk their lives for liberty."

The daring venture shattered widespread stereotypes about African slaves and inspired the broad public support that allowed President Abraham Lincoln to issue the Emancipation Proclamation, freeing the slaves with full United States citizenship.

Both North and South were ravenous for every detail about the intrepid slave, Robert Smalls, who masterminded the daredevil escapade. This is his story.

# 1.

# HOUSE SLAVE AND SAILOR

Although he was born a slave, Robert Smalls was proud of his heritage among the African tribes of Guinea. His mother, Lydia, made certain of that by teaching him that he was the descendant of great warriors. Lydia began her own life on a rice plantation in the Sea Islands off the South Carolina coast. She endured the most brutal cruelties as a field slave in the paddies until her owner, John K. McKee, moved Lydia to work in his home on Prince Street in Beaufort, a sleepy little city on Port Royal Island. Recognizing her high character, natural kindness, and sharp wit, McKee entrusted her with the care of his five children. At age forty-nine she bore her only child, Robert, in a wood-plank slave shack in the McKees' backyard. The McKees were among South Carolina's wealthiest citizens, and the family treated Robert well. When John McKee died in 1848, Robert and his mother became the property of John's eldest son, Henry.

Despite the comparative comfort of their lives as house slaves, Lydia always reminded Robert of the harsh conditions of her early existence. She made sure that Robert never forgot the precariousness of his condition by forcing him to watch slaves being whipped in the streets of Beaufort. She took him to the Beaufort Armory to witness the slave auctions. Robert saw families divided and watched Black people being bought and sold like animals, in leg

1

shackles and neck irons. In this way, Lydia inspired her son with an enduring hunger for freedom.

When Robert was twelve, his master Henry McKee sent him to Charleston, hiring him out as a hotel waiter and then as a lamplighter for the city. His reputation for being a hard worker landed him a job on the Charleston docks as a stevedore, driving the hoisting horses that powered the cranes used to lift heavy objects in the shipyard. Robert's good nature and ingenuity won him a rapid advance to foreman. Recognizing Robert's energy, resourcefulness, and technical abilities, the shipyard owner swiftly promoted him to sailmaker and topsail rigger.

In the warmer months, Robert manned a merchant schooner to the Sea Islands and the Georgia and Carolina coasts. He was soon navigating and handling every kind of boat with such skill and confidence that the ship captains regarded him as one of South Carolina's finest sailors. Although illiterate, he mastered all the elements of sailing. He could read maps and charts, and he understood the currents and the tides. Robert memorized the locations of the channels, bars, and reefs, and the bays and inlets from Charleston to Savannah, Georgia.

Robert's wages legally belonged to his master, but at age eighteen, Robert negotiated with Henry McKee to keep anything he earned over fifteen dollars per month. His sixteen-dollar salary left him one dollar each month for his own pocket. Robert earned extra money performing odd jobs and by the shrewd buying and selling of items during his coastal cruises.

In 1858, at age nineteen, Robert married Hannah Jones, a slave hotel maid owned by Samuel Kingman. Hannah bore a daughter, Elizabeth Lydia, a year later. Since his baby girl was also the property of Kingman, Robert bargained with the master to buy freedom for

Elizabeth and Hannah for eight hundred dollars. By 1861, after nearly four years of hard work, Robert had earned seven hundred dollars, an enormous fortune for a slave. But when Lydia bore him a son, Robert worried that the new baby meant that he'd now have to pay more to purchase his family's freedom. He began to dream of escape.

Robert Smalls had heard through the "slave telegraph" that his mother had been freed with ten thousand other slaves in Port Royal, South Carolina, when the Yankees had captured the island in November. She was now working as a paid cook in Beaufort for the Union army under Major General David Hunter. Robert was determined to move his whole family north.

# 2.

# THE *PLANTER*

———◆———

A YEAR EARLIER, ROBERT HAD HIRED ON AS A SAILOR ON THE *PLANTER*, Captain John Ferguson's high-pressure side-wheeler designed to haul cotton. Ferguson had chartered the *Planter* and her civilian crew to the Confederate navy, which had outfitted her as a gunship with a cannon in her bow and a howitzer astern. A large freighter, 147 feet long and 50 feet abeam, the *Planter*'s broad deck could carry a thousand troops and their gear. The *Planter*'s shallow five-foot draft made her ideal for transporting men and supplies through coastal South Carolina's labyrinth of estuaries, tributaries, and rivers.

As Charleston prepared for a Yankee attack, the *Planter* patrolled the harbor, placing mines and carrying troops and armaments to the outlying forts and batteries.

Soon after Robert hired on as a deckhand, his perfect knowledge of the bays and shoals persuaded the Confederate officers to promote him first to head crewman and then to ship's pilot.

One day, a slave sailor joked to Robert that they should steal the *Planter*. Smalls hushed his friend, whispering that the idea was more than a joke, and ordered him to never again mention it aboard the ship. After work, the two men began feeling out the other Black crew members: two engineers and four other sailors and deckhands. They decided not to include one of the slaves, a fifth deckhand, who nobody trusted.

The slaves gathered late at night to plan their dangerous scheme by candlelight at Robert's house. They agreed to be ready at a moment's notice and left it to Robert to decide when to move. All the conspirators promised to obey his orders.

On some nights the *Planter*'s White officers would leave their ship in Smalls' care, moored to the wharf adjacent to Confederate headquarters. Twenty-one marines stood on the pier tightly guarding the *Planter*. On the afternoon of May 12, 1862, Confederate soldiers and stevedores loaded the steamship with six heavy guns and several hundred pounds of ammunition for shipment to the harbor fortifications. The guns included two magnificent cannons captured from the Union army following the surrender at Fort Sumter. Local ironsmiths had finally repaired the Yankee guns from the damage they suffered during the fierce battle, and the Rebels were excited to deploy the big artillery pieces for their own cause. Thinking to himself that these weapons would make a fine gift for "Uncle Abe," Smalls deliberately slowed down the loading process so that the cargo could not be delivered that day.

At sundown, the Confederate captain, C.J. Relyea, his mate, and his chief engineer announced that they were going ashore to spend the night. Ambling down the gangplank, Captain Relyea ordered Robert to ready the ship to shove off at 6 a.m. on the high tide. "Aye, aye, sir," Smalls replied. The moment the sailors were out of sight, Smalls spread the word among his crew to be ready that night.

The slaves sent messages to their wives and children. That

evening, as Charleston slept, two women and their little ones stole away from their masters' homes. Arriving at the port in the darkness, they hid aboard a merchant ship moored to a nearby dock under the care of a slave sailor who was a friend of Smalls' and who would join the adventure.

# 3.

# SAILING TO FREEDOM

———•———

NONE OF THE CONPIRATORS WOULD SLEEP THAT NIGHT. AROUND 3 A.M., Smalls and his men slipped past the Confederate marines patrolling the wharf and boarded the *Planter*. Robert broke into the pilot house and donned Captain Relyea's uniform, pistols, and his broad-brimmed straw hat. Before starting the engines, the slaves quietly swore to one another that if they were caught, they would detonate the ship's explosives, sink the *Planter*, and die fighting.

Knowing the captain and mates might return as early as 5 a.m., the renegade slaves fired up the steam generators at 3:30 a.m. The roar seemed loud enough to waken the whole city. Thick smoke from the stacks swept down onto Charleston. A terrifying eternity passed as the eight men waited for the steam pressure to build. They prayed that the armed Confederate soldier on the wharf would not sound the alert, or that the howling, billowing turbines would not tip off the captain or cause someone to sound the fire alarms.

When the pressure was sufficient, Smalls ordered his men to loosen the lines and raise the Confederate flag. Then he blew the *Planter*'s whistle to signal they were leaving the wharf. Smalls stood beside the wheelhouse, wearing the captain's hat and uniform with his arms on his hips, elbows spread wide, imitating the captain's well-known posture. Shielded by darkness, the *Planter* steamed slowly across the harbor to the dock where the women

9

and children were hiding. As soon as they climbed safely aboard, Smalls turned his ship and sailed leisurely seaward, passing six fortified Confederate checkpoints bristling with deadly guns. At each fort, Smalls blew the *Planter*'s horns according to the coded signals, which he knew by heart.

The tide was against them, and they did not reach Fort Sumter till daylight. As they steamed past the great citadel, Smalls fetched up his collar and pulled the straw hat low to hide the Black skin of his face. He pulled the rope, making two long whistles and a short jerk—the final code for gunboats leaving the harbor. The officer on watch signaled him to pass, and Robert, cool as ice, steamed at a crawl directly under Fort Sumter's steep stone walls and powerful cannons. In that moment of greatest peril, he prayed to himself, "*Lord, you brought Moses and the Israelites from slavery, safely across the Red Sea. Please carry your children now to the promised land of freedom!*"

As soon as she was beyond Sumter's guns, Smalls buried the *Planter*'s throttle and changed course, racing for the open sea and the Union blockade ships. Through the morning mist, Robert spotted on the horizon the silhouettes of ten warships from the federal squadron. Setting course for the nearest federal gunboat, Robert ordered his men to strike the Confederate colors and haul up a bedsheet he'd stripped off one of the bunks.

From the crow's nest on the federal frigate *Onward*, a lookout spotted the Confederate gunship coming at full speed toward them out of the fog and sounded the alarm. Thinking it meant to ram them, the *Onward*'s captain, F. J. Nickerson, brought *Onward* about to meet a hostile attack with his broadside guns. Just as he was about to order a cannon barrage, a sailor shouted that the ship was flying a white flag. Instructing his gunners to hold their fire, Captain Nickerson signaled the *Planter* to pull in astern.

Captain Nickerson was shocked to see a dashing young Black man wearing the Rebel captain's hat, dressed elegantly in a white shirt and Confederate officer's waistcoat, leaning confidently against the *Planter*'s gunwale. Doffing his hat expansively, the handsome youth saluted and called to the captain, "Good morning, sir! I've brought you some of the old United States' guns."

On the *Planter*'s deck, eight triumphant Black men were cheering wildly. When Captain Nickerson boarded the *Planter*, the exultant crew engulfed him, pleading that he give them an American flag to raise above their prize.

As they hoisted the Stars and Stripes, five more Black passengers emerged from the *Planter*'s hatches— two women and three children. Smalls' wife, Hannah, had tears of joy flowing down her cheeks. Raising their infant son, Robert, in her arms, she told him to gaze at the American flag. "It means freedom, child! Oh, Robert, it means freedom!"

Captain Nickerson greeted them cordially. After hearing Robert Smalls'

story, Nickerson sent him to retell it to the blockade squadron commander, who decided to send the *Planter* with its crew of escaped slaves under Union commanders sixty miles up the coast to Port Royal, the headquarters of the Union army and fleet. Their families would go to Beaufort, where they would be safe for the remainder of the war.

# 4.

# BACK ON SHORE

———•———

BACK IN CHARLESTON, THE CONFEDERATE COMMANDER, BRIGADIER
General Roswell S. Ripley, was astonished that morning when
his troops told him that the *Planter* had vanished from her berth
directly in front of Ripley's headquarters on the Charleston wharf.

The Confederate troops who had guarded the *Planter* that night
said that they had seen Captain Relyea in his familiar straw hat
standing at the rail in the darkness as the ship fired her engines
at 3:30 a.m. and then steamed off, flying the
Confederate flag. The guards were not
surprised to see her go, since they
had been told she was scheduled
to sail early.

They watched her land
briefly at a dock across the
harbor. Then her whistle blew,
and she steamed unhurriedly
toward Fort Sumter, where
the officer in charge received
her salute, and thinking her on
guard duty, signaled her to pass
into the outer harbor. Only one
of the *Planter*'s original crew of nine

slaves remained ashore. He genuinely seemed to know nothing. At first the Confederates found it unthinkable that slaves could have commandeered their finest vessel. General Ripley only accepted the shocking truth when, using a telescope, he frantically scanned the horizon and found the *Planter* anchored between two federal frigates out beyond the sandbars.

The Charleston press called the *Planter*'s loss "criminal negligence" and blamed its Confederate officers for "disgusting treachery" in allowing "one of the most shameful events of this or any other war." Fuming over the abduction in the Confederate capital of Richmond, Virginia, General Robert E. Lee ordered swift punishment for the guilty parties. Captain Relyea and his mates were court-martialed, fined, and imprisoned.

Tales of the daring takeover triggered weeks of celebration in Northern states. Congress passed and President Lincoln signed a bill awarding Smalls and his crew half the value of the ship. Calling Smalls' leadership "one of the coolest and most gallant naval acts of war," the navy's grateful commander, Admiral Samuel F. Du Pont, asked that a prize of $5,000 be awarded to Smalls and that $15,000 be split among the eight other men and two women who had played key roles in the adventure.

# 5.

# THE BATTLE FOR STONO INLET

WITH THE YANKEE OFFICERS ABOARD AND SMALLS ACTING AS PILOT, THE *Planter* arrived at Union headquarters in Port Royal at 10:30 that evening. The Union fleet commander, Admiral Du Pont, was anxious to meet Smalls.

After retelling his story, Smalls gave Admiral Du Pont a book he had managed to purloin, containing all the secret codes and signals of the Confederate navy. The Confederate code book allowed the blockade vessels to decipher the various signal flags that were raised by the Confederate forts and batteries across Charleston Harbor.

Admiral Du Pont was astonished that Smalls had memorized the location, size, and power of Confederate fortifications throughout coastal South Carolina and knew the exact locations where the Confederates had placed their mines and torpedoes in the creeks and tributaries to foil Union attackers.

Best of all, Smalls reported in great detail the movements of all the Confederate soldiers and arms. He told Admiral Du Pont that the Rebel army had secretly abandoned its fortification, guarding the northern approach to Charleston at Stono Inlet. Admiral Du Pont recognized that this information would allow the Union army to retake Charleston by land.

The Union army, under Major General David Hunter, had been stalled at Port Royal mainly due to a lack of vessels needed to transport the army among the complex waterways of the Carolina coast. Du Pont sent a dispatch to General Hunter with Smalls' information about Stono Inlet. In his dispatch, he described Smalls as "a man of superior intelligence" and urged that Smalls' information be treated with utmost importance. Acting on Smalls' tip, General Hunter immediately began moving his army down the coast for a ground assault on Charleston. The *Planter* was a godsend to General Hunter. His army had been badly in need of a shallow-water ship. Here was the perfect craft for ferrying the army through the rivers and shoals of South Carolina's coastal archipelagos. And best of all, in Smalls, they now had a master sailor with intricate knowledge of the local waterways. General Hunter asked Robert Smalls to join the expedition as pilot.

Smalls steered troops up the coast for the Union navy and led three federal gunships across the Stono Inlet shoals, guiding the attack on the fort. His detailed knowledge of the sounds and rivers helped the Union army take Stono Inlet and establish Yankee fortifications. The U.S. Navy secretary credited Smalls with making the victory possible.

Unfortunately, bureaucratic delays by the Union army prevented General Hunter from moving against Charleston. The stall gave the Rebels the chance to fortify new defenses for the city, and the Yankees dropped their planned assault for the moment. Nevertheless, the Union victory at Stono Inlet proved a turning point in the battle for Charleston, and Stono would be an important base in future operations.

# 6.

# CAPTAIN ROBERT SMALLS

———◆———

DESPITE THE LEGISLATION SIGNED BY LINCOLN AND THE EFFORTS BY Admiral Du Pont to award Smalls and the *Planter*'s crew their fair reward of $20,000 for delivering the gunship, mean-spirited accountants in the Department of War, not wanting former slaves to receive such a "fortune," reduced the total payout to $4,500, with $1,400 going to Smalls.

If he felt bitter, Smalls never showed it. For the next three years he continued to serve the Union army with rare distinction. He piloted the *Planter* and other ships through seventeen naval battles, always displaying courage and daring. Each time he engaged the enemy, Smalls knew he risked far more than did the White sailors he fought alongside. He and his crew of former slaves would face brutal torture, maiming, and death, if they ever fell into the hands of the Confederates.

On April 7, 1863, the Union command gave Smalls the honor of piloting one of the world's first ironclads—the *Keokuk*—during the naval assault on Charleston. Although the Union attempt to recapture Fort Sumter failed, Smalls distinguished himself with legendary coolness during the battle. When the fleet stalled with its flagship run aground, Smalls guided the *Keokuk* around the stranded ships for a direct attack on the fort. There he came under hot fire from the Confederate guns. Cannonade blasts struck the *Keokuk* ninety-six times, with nineteen shots at or below the waterline. A shell burst damaged Smalls' eyes and killed his first mate. Despite his injuries, Smalls steered his crew to safety, unloading them to a rescue ship just minutes before the *Keokuk* sank upright.

In May 1863, Smalls was back on the *Planter*, piloting for a Yankee captain on a supply mission on the Kiawah River near Charleston. They were carrying ammunition to an isolated Union army division on Morris Island and bringing badly needed rations to the hungry troops. Within view of the Yankee soldiers, a Confederate warship ambushed the *Planter*, forcing her between three Confederate forts where Rebel gunners raked her with a withering crossfire from three sides. The fierce fusillade tore into the *Planter*'s smokestack and wheelhouse. Fire from short rounds splintered her deck. The screaming shells and smoke panicked the captain, who ordered Smalls to beach the *Planter* and surrender. Smalls defiantly refused the order. "Not by a damned sight will I beach this boat for you," he shouted above the blast. As the captain ran below to hide, Smalls took command of the ship, sailing the *Planter* through the maelstrom of smoke and hot lead safely to the Union battery. Thousands of Union troops, desperate for supplies, had watched her run the savage gauntlet. Now they awaited her, cheering wildly from the landing. Major General Quincy Gillmore boarded

the tattered *Planter* to congratulate its commander and crew for extraordinary bravery and seamanship. After dismissing the captain for cowardice, Gillmore promoted Robert to captain on the spot, making Robert Smalls the first Black captain of a United States vessel in the history of our nation. He served at that rank for the remainder of the war.

# 7.

# ABE LINCOLN

EVEN AS HE WAS FIGHTING IN THE CIVIL WAR, ROBERT PLAYED AN important role in the emancipation of Black slaves.

In August 1862, at the request of General Hunter, Robert traveled to Washington, D.C. with the abolitionist leader Reverend Mansfield French. In Washington, Robert met with President Abraham Lincoln; his secretary of war, Edwin Stanton; and his treasury secretary, Salmon Chase. Smalls urged the President to arm the thousands of Black slaves who had been abandoned by their masters when Port Royal's Rebel population fled before the Union army. With charm and eloquence, Smalls told the President that former slaves were anxious, able, and badly needed to protect the Union-occupied regions of the South from Rebel raiders. His eloquent plea convinced Lincoln, and Smalls returned to Port Royal with the President's permission to enlist 5,000 Black men as soldiers in the Union army. Smalls had played a critical role in shattering the color barrier that had kept Black people from military service.

Robert was considered a prince by Black freedmen. They greeted him as a hero everywhere he went. Despite his inability to read or write, Robert became an articulate and charismatic public speaker. Abolitionists sent Robert on a speaking tour to raise money

at Black and White church meetings for the Union cause. In 1862, the Black community of New York City gathered at Shiloh Church to present Robert with a massive gold medal struck in his honor. The medal showed a relief of Robert and the *Planter* in the port of Charleston. The assembly praised Smalls for his "heroism, love of liberty, and his patriotism." Deafening cheers shook the roof of the famous church when he appeared with his wife and his little son, Robert. Standing at the lectern, Robert spoke with modesty, nobility, and confidence for the cause of freedom.

In May of 1864, a convention of Black freedmen and White people in Beaufort selected Robert as a delegate to the Republican National Convention, making him one of the first four Black men to serve in this capacity. But Smalls was still preoccupied with fighting the war.

# 8.

# PHILADELPHIA

———◆———

ROBERT'S COMMANDER HAD SENT HIM TO PHILADELPHIA TO REFIT and overhaul the battle-battered *Planter*. Jealous of Smalls' success and speedy promotions, a small group of Union officers conspired to destroy Robert's reputation. They arranged that he be ordered to personally sail the *Planter* north unassisted. They were confident that the illiterate former slave could never navigate the impossibly intricate channels and strong currents of Cape Hatteras, the Chesapeake Bay, and the Delaware River. They fully expected him to founder his ship and then be drummed out of the service. Smalls, however, was overjoyed by the challenge and made the trip in just three days. Once again, he had astonished his doubters.

In Philadelphia, Robert confidently supervised the *Planter*'s refitting. In his spare time, he worked hard learning to read and write, a privilege forbidden to slaves under South Carolina law. Of the *Planter*'s six Black crew members, only one, John Smalls (no relation to Robert), the engineer, was literate. When a reporter asked him how he had learned to read, he replied, "I stole it at night, sir."

Robert continued working to support newly freed slaves in the South. With his customary dignity, he also struck a blow for equality in Philadelphia. Returning home one rainy day from the shipyard, Robert and a friend had just taken their seats on a city streetcar when a conductor directed the two Black men to move to the streetcar's outside platform. The conductor explained that city laws prohibited Black people from sitting in streetcars and ordered them to make way for White passengers. Smalls, instead, disembarked and walked home in the rain. That humiliation to the hero of Charleston received national publicity. The public outcry inspired Philadelphians to repeal the city's race laws. The "City of Brotherly Love" finally integrated its streetcars in 1867.

# 9.

# HOME TO BEAUFORT

———◆———

BY THE WINTER OF 1864, SMALLS AND THE *PLANTER* WERE BACK IN action, supporting General William Tecumseh Sherman in his march across the South. After Sherman's army conquered Atlanta and Savannah, Robert helped move Union troops up the coast into the Carolinas. The Yankees took Charleston on February 17, 1865.

When Charleston surrendered, Smalls escorted General Rufus B. Saxton into the city, where adoring mobs of cheering Black people greeted them. On the outskirts of the crowd, standing with a small group of White people, Smalls spotted his old boss, Captain John Ferguson, the *Planter*'s original owner. Pulling General Saxton through the crowd, Smalls introduced him to Captain Ferguson, a gesture that testified to his changed status and equality.

After the war, Smalls returned to Beaufort, and using his congressional prize money, he bought the old McKee estate where he had been born. He would live there for the rest of his life. Working hard, he became a successful businessman and acquired extensive property and buildings around Beaufort. But he devoted most of his energies to public service. He labored to build Beaufort and Port Royal into communities where both races could live together, prosper, and flourish. Robert joined the South Carolina Militia, and he was soon promoted to major general, the militia's top commander.

As militia commander, Robert distinguished himself by peacefully settling a violent strike by rice-field workers. During this episode, he no doubt recalled his mother's tales of the brutality of South Carolina's rice plantations. Robert negotiated with the striking workers in Gullah, the language of the Sea Island slaves, which he had learned as a boy. Gullah was a rich mixture of West African languages and seventeenth-century English. The workers told him of their terrible mistreatment and the cruelty of the plantation owners, who used a payment system designed to return them to the status of slaves. Afterward, Robert kept his promise to the workers by persuading South Carolina's governor to pass laws making such mistreatment illegal.

Robert built the first public school in South Carolina and became the leading advocate for public school education across the state. He was one of the founders of the Republican Party in South Carolina. This was the party of Lincoln, who, in Smalls' words, had "unshackled the necks of four million human beings."

Robert remained popular among both the Black and White citizens of Beaufort, and in 1868, Beaufort's citizens elected Robert to represent them in the South Carolina Legislature. That year, voters also chose Robert as a delegate to draft the state's constitution. The document granted equal rights to all South Carolina's citizens. Beaufort sent Robert to the state senate in 1870. And in 1874, the town's citizens elected Robert Smalls as their United States congressman. He served five terms in the House of Representatives, longer than any Black person until the 1950s.

While in the House, he authored and passed a bill requiring equal rights for both races on trains. Prior to that law, railroads assigned Black people the worst seats or forced them to stand. Robert also fought to integrate the armed services and to grant women the right

to vote. He used his political power to fight corruption and waste in government. He fought for fair elections and battled to reform the tax system, which favored the rich and punished the poor. Robert used his personal wealth and political connections to provide jobs and care for many poor people, both Black and White, including his former masters, the McKee family, who were now destitute, having fallen on hard times. For fifty years, Robert Smalls was the most powerful Black man in South Carolina and a fierce fighter for American democracy and for the rights of the poor, women, and people of all races.

# 10.

# THE CONFEDERACY RISES AGAIN

UP UNTIL 1876, THE REPUBLICAN PARTY, WHICH CONTROLLED CONGRESS and the presidency, fiercely protected the civil rights of former slaves in the southern states. Most important among those guarantees was the right to vote. Since Black people outnumbered White people by nearly two to one in South Carolina, many Black officials now held power in state and national government.

But former Confederates were determined to deprive South Carolina's Black people of their newfound rights and restore the social order of the prewar South. They controlled the Democratic Party across the South, and by 1876, they began gaining power nationally. At the same time, the Republican Party began deserting the Southern freedmen. The industrial revolution was spreading, and large, powerful industrialists known as "robber barons" were using their wealth to gain control of both political parties. Tempted by that easy money, the Republican Party embraced the great corporations, abandoned its idealism, and left the freed slaves to the mercy of their former masters. Republicans now saw democracy and racial equality as "bad for business."

The old-guard Confederates now busied themselves with the tasks of reversing the reforms that Robert Smalls had helped win for his fellow freedmen. White supremacist Democrats openly stole elections and threw out most of South Carolina's Black elected officials. To discourage Black people from voting, the Ku Klux Klan made lynchings, beatings, and murder a daily occurrence. Wholesale voter fraud marred nearly every election in the state. "We stuffed the ballot boxes," South Carolina Senator and former governor Ben Tillman would boast to the United States Senate in 1900. "We shot Negroes; we are not ashamed of it!"

Beaufort, where Black people outnumbered White people seven to one, was one of the last remaining pockets of Black political power. Because Robert also enjoyed the support of many of Beaufort's White residents, he was able to hold his seat long after the white supremacists had forced other Black elected officials out of office. Nevertheless, Robert was under constant attack by the old Confederate guard, who still referred to him bitterly as "the boat thief." The Ku Klux Klan lynched Smalls' supporters, threatened his life and property, and turned every Election Day into a circus of violence, murder, and fraud designed to keep his supporters away from the polls.

In 1886, after Robert had served ten years in Congress, white supremacists from the old Confederacy finally stole the election from him.

Republicans in Congress joined with Democrats to prevent Robert from regaining his seat. Robert's enemies also had him imprisoned on phony charges of taking bribes; the governor pardoned Robert and released him from prison when his supporters proved those charges false.

In 1895, Senator Ben Tillman called a state constitutional convention for the express purpose of robbing Black South Carolinians of the right to vote. Tillman intended to repeal the model constitution that Smalls had helped to draft in 1869 and permanently relegate Black people to second-class citizenship.

Only six Black people attended the convention, all but one from Beaufort. Robert Smalls was their star. He delivered a series of extraordinary speeches at the South Carolina Constitutional Convention in an unsuccessful attempt to prevent the disenfranchisement of his race. Through breathtaking passion and intelligence, he nearly succeeded. His eloquent plea against bigotry and in support of America's promise of a truly representative democracy nearly persuaded even the hard-line white supremacists, who now controlled the state. A contemporary writer called Smalls "a potent force in the convention."

"The ringing speeches made by him were masterpieces of impregnable logic, consecutive reasoning, bitter sarcasm, and fiery invectives. . . . His arguments were simply unanswerable, and the keenness of his wit, the cleverness of his arrangements, and the persistence with which he routed his opponents from one subterfuge to another astounded the convention."

But in the end, Tillman and the forces of hatred were too powerful. Their new constitution robbed almost all of South Carolina's Black people of their right to vote and the other rights of American citizens. In South Carolina and across the South, Black people would not regain those rights until the Civil Rights Movement of the 1960s.

Despite those setbacks, Robert Smalls refused to stop fighting for the principles of democracy and freedom. He campaigned across the country against South Carolina's unfair and undemocratic laws, always appealing to America's idealism, her decency, and sense of fairness. He remained devoted to the ideals of an America that treated all women and men fairly, regardless of their race.

His noble character had won him many permanent friends, and he never relinquished his optimistic outlook. In 1890, he accepted an appointment from Republican President Benjamin Harrison as customs collector of the port of Beaufort. Robert held the post for twenty years. He managed the affairs of the customs office cleanly and professionally and left an impeccable record of honesty and good management. In 1900, Congress finally gave him the additional $5,000 that was his rightful reward for capturing the *Planter*. In 1913, Democrats took the White House and fired him from the customs-office job. He left without bitterness. Robert died two years later in 1915 and went before his Maker beloved by his fellow citizens. His funeral was the largest in the history of the city. Thousands of grieving South Carolinians openly wept as a Black chorus sang Robert's favorite spiritual, "Shall We Meet Beyond the River?"

# AFTERWORD

ROBERT SMALLS WAS A TRUE AMERICAN PATRIOT. DESPITE THE BURDENS America had laid upon him, he never stopped loving our country. Smalls believed in the "inherent justice" of American democracy and in the principles espoused in the Declaration of Independence. To him the American dream meant building a nation that was a praiseworthy example to all humanity, reflecting the best of the human character, and our loftiest values and ideals.

He played an important role in making America—for a short time—a true representative democracy for the first time in her history. Thanks in part to his efforts, between 1865 and 1876, for a brief shining moment, America came close to achieving her promise.

In 1876, the forces of ignorance, hatred, and greed eclipsed that America, which had seemed so much within reach during the decade after the Civil War. Always optimistic about human decency, Smalls was a practical realist who knew that democracy and freedom could never be taken for granted. His life was a noble, dignified, and courageous struggle for those ideals, a struggle that only ended on the day he died.

But Smalls' spirit rose again fifty years later to invigorate and inspire the souls and voices of a new generation of Black leaders like Martin Luther King, Jr., who would finally guide America toward keeping its great covenant with history.

# BIBLIOGRAPHY

## BOOKS

Billingsley, Andrew. *Yearning to Breathe Free: Robert Smalls of South Carolina and His Families.*
Columbia, S.C.: University of South Carolina Press, 2007.

Brown, Susan T. *Robert Smalls Sails to Freedom.* Minneapolis: Millbrook Press, 2005.
(written for young people)

Cooper, Michael L. *From Slave to Civil War Hero: The Life and Times of Robert Smalls.*
New York: Dutton Juvenile, 1994. (written for young people)

Meriwether, Louise. *The Freedom Ship of Robert Smalls.* Englewood Cliffs: Prentice Hall, 1971.
(written for young people)

Miller, Edward A. *Gullah Statesman: Robert Smalls from Slavery to Congress, 1839-1915.*
Columbia, S.C.: University of South Carolina Press, 1995.

Sterling, Dorothy. *Captain of the* Planter: *The Story of Robert Smalls.* New York: Doubleday, 1958.
(written for young people)

Uya, Okon Edet. *From Slavery to Public Service: Robert Smalls, 1839-1915.* New York:
Oxford University Press, 1971.

## ARTICLES

*Harper's Weekly.* "Robert Smalls: Captain of the Gun-Boat 'Planter,'" June 14, 1862.
See http://www.sonofthesouth.net/leefoundation/civil-war/1862/june/robert-smalls-planter.htm.